A New True Book

MAPS AND GLOBES

By Ray Broekel

This "true book" was prepared
under the direction of
Illa Podendorf,
formerly with the Laboratory School,
University of Chicago

CHILDRENS PRESS, CHICAGO

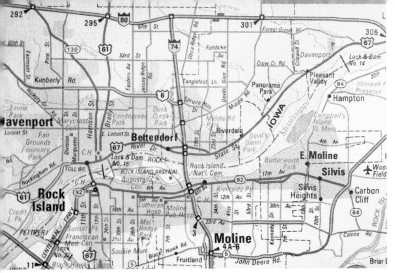

Road map

PHOTO CREDITS

Lynn M. Stone—11, 36

Joseph A. Dichello—10

Reinhard Brucker—2, 4 (2 photos),
15, 22, 30, 32, 35, 39 (right)

Bob Ulm—19, 24, 25

Len Meents—6, 13, 14, 18, 20, 26, 27,
33, 37

NASA—39 (left)

© Copyright by Rand McNally &
Company—8, 29 (2 photos), 31, 44

Hillstrom Stock Photos—© W.S.
Nawrocki, cover, 41

Don & Pat Valenti—43

Library of Congress Cataloging in Publication Data

Broekel, Ray.
  Maps and globes.

  (A New true book)
  Includes index.
  Summary: Briefly discusses different types of maps
and globes and explains such map-related terms as symbol,
key, direction, and scale.
  1. Maps—Juvenile literature. 2. Globes—Juvenile
literature. [1. Maps. 2. Globes] I. Title.
II. Series.
GA105.6.B76 1983   912   83-7509
ISBN 0-516-01695-4   AACR2

11 12 13 14 15 16 17 18 19 20 R 02 01 00 99 98 97 96 95 94 93

TABLE OF CONTENTS

Road map (right)
and street map
(below)

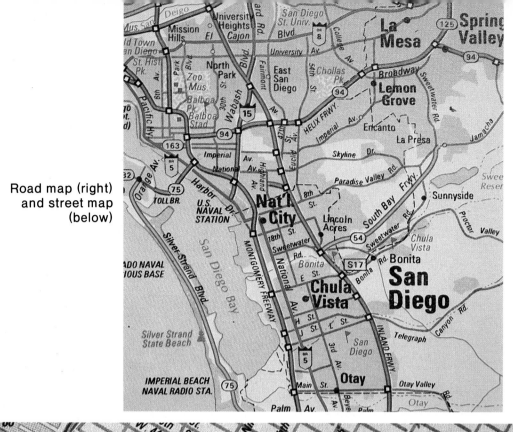

WHAT IS A MAP?

A map is a drawing of a place. The drawing shows where things are.

A map can show the things in a room such as a classroom.

A map can show the houses, buildings, and streets in a town.

A map can show the towns, lakes, and

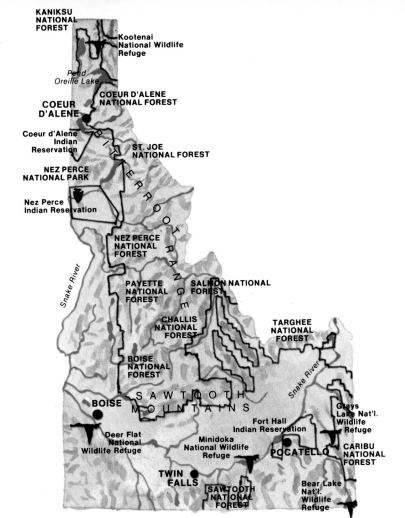

Map of national parks, forests, and wildlife refuges in the state of Idaho

KANIKSU NATIONAL FOREST

Kootenai National Wildlife Refuge

Pend Oreille Lake

COEUR D'ALENE

COEUR D'ALENE NATIONAL FOREST

Coeur d'Alene Indian Reservation

ST. JOE NATIONAL FOREST

NEZ PERCE NATIONAL PARK

Nez Perce Indian Reservation

NEZ PERCE NATIONAL FOREST

Snake River

BITTERROOT RANGE

PAYETTE NATIONAL FOREST

SALMON NATIONAL FOREST

CHALLIS NATIONAL FOREST

TARGHEE NATIONAL FOREST

BOISE NATIONAL FOREST

S A W T O O T H   M O U N T A I N S

BOISE

Snake River

Grays Lake Nat'l. Wildlife Refuge

Deer Flat National Wildlife Refuge

Fort Hall Indian Reservation

Minidoka National Wildlife Refuge

POCATELLO

CARIBU NATIONAL FOREST

TWIN FALLS

SAWTOOTH NATIONAL FOREST

Bear Lake Nat'l. Wildlife Refuge

mountains in a state or country.

A map also can show many other things about the world we live in.

MAP SYMBOLS

A symbol is a figure that stands for something else.

A map symbol for a railroad track is a black line with short lines cutting across it. +++++++++++++++

Color can also be used for a symbol. A symbol for a river is a blue line that bends as the river does.

Symbols are used on different kinds of maps. Some maps are called charts.

Potomac River
Baltimore
Parkersburg
Cumberland
MD
DOVER
DEL
WASHINGTON D.C.
WEST VIRGINIA
ANNAPOLIS
Chesapeake Bay
Louisville
Lexington
CHARLESTON
VIRGINIA
RICHMOND
CAPE CHARLES
FRANKFORT
Shenandoah Nat'l Park
Norfolk
Owensboro
KENTUCKY
James Lynchburg R.
Roanoke
Danville
Roanoke R.
Albemarle Sd.
Ohio River
MAMMOTH CAVE NAT'L PARK
L. Cumberland
Pamlico Sd.
Paducah
Cumberland R.
PLATEAU
RALEIGH
CAPE HATTERAS
Kentucky Lake
NASHVILLE
Knoxville
NORTH CAROLINA
Neuse R.
Cumberland R.
MT. MITCHELL 6,684 FT.
MAGAZINE MTN. 2,823 FT.
TENNESSEE
Chickamauga L.
GREAT SMOKY MTS. NAT'L PARK
Asheville
Charlotte
CAPE LOOKOUT
White
Ft. Smith
River
Memphis
Chattanooga
Tennessee R.
Greenville
Cape Fear R.
Wilmington
ARKANSAS
Wilson Lake
Greenwood
SOUTH
CAPE FEAR
HOT SPRINGS NAT'L PARK
LITTLE ROCK
Guntersville Lake
Hartwell Res.
Clark-Hill Res.
L. Murray
COLUMBIA
OUACHITA MTS
Pine Bluff
Smith Res.
Birmingham
CAROLINA
L. Marion
L. Moultrie
CAPE ROMAIN
Ouachita R.
YAZOO RIVER BASIN
MISSISSIPPI
Tombigbee R.
ATLANTA
Augusta
Charleston
Texarkana
ALABAMA
GEORGIA
Savannah R.
Atlantic Ocean
Shreveport
JACKSON
Meridian
MONTGOMERY
Columbus
Oconee R.
Altamaha R.
Savannah
Red River
Martin Lake
Ocmulgee R.
LOUISIANA
Alexandria
Chattahoochee R.
Albany
Flint R.
Alapaha R.
Jacksonville
Sabine River
Pearl River
BATON ROUGE
Mobile
Alabama R.
F
L
O
St. Johns
Mississippi River
L. Pontchartrain
Pensacola
TALLAHASSEE
R
Daytona Beach
New Orleans
CAPE SAN BLAS
Apalachicola River
Apalachee Bay
I
D
St. Johns River
CAPE KENNEDY
Atchafalaya Bay
Mississippi River Delta
L. George
A
Orlando
Gulf   of   Mexico
Tampa
Lake Okeechobee
W. Palm Beach
THE EVERGLADES
EVERGLADES NAT'L PARK
Miami
CAPE SABLE
Key West

Evergreen Trees
Deciduous Trees
Shrub
Grass

✪ Capitals
● Cities

1 inch = 175 Statute Miles
Miles 0 25 50 75 100 125 150

Lambert Conformal Conic Projection

®RMCN

®Rand McNally & Co., R.L. 83-S-109

An outline map is used for charts. An outline shows the boundaries of something. The outline may be of a room, a town, a state, or a country. Then symbols are put onto the map to tell a story.

This outline map shows a group of states. The symbols for state capitals are black stars. The symbols for other cities are black circles. The symbols for state boundaries are red lines.

MAP KEYS

A map has a key, or legend. The key shows the symbols used on the map.

Different symbols are used for different kinds of maps.

A road-map key will have symbols for things such as highways and paved roads.

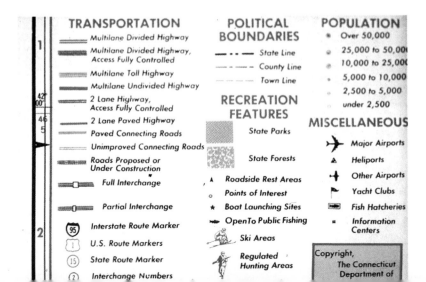

TRANSPORTATION

Multilane Divided Highway

Multilane Divided Highway, Access Fully Controlled

Multilane Toll Highway

Multilane Undivided Highway

2 Lane Highway, Access Fully Controlled

2 Lane Paved Highway

Paved Connecting Roads

Unimproved Connecting Roads

Roads Proposed or Under Construction

Full Interchange

Partial Interchange

Interstate Route Marker

U.S. Route Markers

State Route Marker

Interchange Numbers

POLITICAL BOUNDARIES

State Line

County Line

Town Line

RECREATION FEATURES

State Parks

State Forests

Roadside Rest Areas

Points of Interest

Boat Launching Sites

Open To Public Fishing

Ski Areas

Regulated Hunting Areas

POPULATION

Over 50,000

25,000 to 50,000

10,000 to 25,000

5,000 to 10,000

2,500 to 5,000

under 2,500

MISCELLANEOUS

Major Airports

Heliports

Other Airports

Yacht Clubs

Fish Hatcheries

Information Centers

Copyright, The Connecticut Department of

MAP EXPLANATION

HIGHWAY MARKERS

INTER-STATE 75   U.S. 27   STATE AND PROVINCIAL 49   CO. C38   TRANS-CANADA ✚

ROAD CLASSIFICATIONS

CONTROLLED ACCESS DIVIDED HIGHWAYS
(Entrance and Exit only at Interchanges)
Interchanges

TOLL HIGHWAYS

OTHER DIVIDED HIGHWAYS

PRINCIPAL THROUGH HIGHWAYS
Paved

OTHER HIGHWAYS
Paved   Gravel

LOCAL ROADS In unfamiliar areas inquire locally before using these roads   Paved   Gravel   Dirt

MILEAGES

MILEAGE BETWEEN TOWNS AND JUNCTIONS   3 4

MILEAGE BETWEEN DOTS   35

LONG DISTANCE MILEAGES SHOWN IN RED

SPECIAL FEATURES

STATE PARKS
With Campsites 🌲   Without Campsites △

RECREATION AREAS
With Campsites ▲   Without Campsites △

PORTS OF ENTRY
Open 24 Hours ✗   Inquire Locally ✗

SELECTED REST AREAS ✗

POINTS OF INTEREST ▣

SCHEDULED AIRLINE STOPS ✈

MILITARY AIRPORTS ✈

OTHER AIRPORTS ✈

SKI AREAS ⛷

BOAT RAMPS ◂

TOURIST INFORMATION ✪

Different colors can be used as symbols in a key. The colors are shown in little boxes or circles in the key.

Many things can be shown in a color-key map.

DIRECTION

On a map the main directions are called cardinal directions. They are north, south, east, and west.

Found between the cardinal directions are intermediate directions. They are northeast, northwest, southeast, and southwest.

Direction can be shown on maps in different ways.

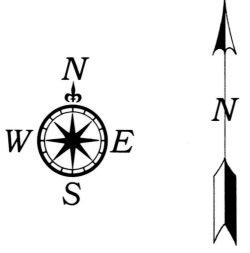

A simple way to show direction is to use an arrow that points north.

Sometimes an N will be shown with the arrow.

A map may have a circle on it showing the cardinal directions. The letters N, E, S, and W are placed at each cardinal direction end.

On some maps a symbol called a compass rose is used. It shows both cardinal and intermediate directions. North is always at the top, even if letters are not used.

SCALE

To read a map you need to know scale.

Scale is a system by which real distances are shown by much smaller distances.

Scale is given in a corner of a map. It may be in the English or the metric system.

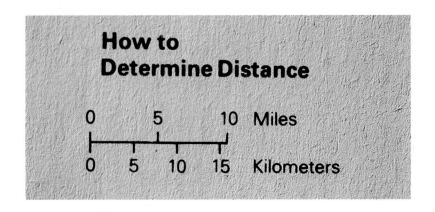

How to Determine Distance

0   5   10 Miles

0   5   10   15 Kilometers

A ruler is used to read scale on a map. Scale may be 1 inch=10 miles. Or 3 millimeters=6 kilometers.

To show more land on a map, make a small-scale map. One inch may be equal to 100 miles. Or 1 millimeter may be equal to 50 kilometers.

Scale can change from one map to another. It depends on how much land is shown.

A MAP KEY NUMBER SYSTEM

Some maps have a map key that uses numbers or letters. It is used to find different things on the map.

MAP KEY

Administration Buildings, C2
Brown House, B5
County Courthouse, A1
Education Building, B4
First Methodist Church, A4
Governor's House, B1

Hill Street, A4&5
Historical Society, A2
Jefferson High School, A4
Morgan Hospital, C4
Natural History Building, C3
Public Library, B2

Remmer House, C1
Shopping Center, C5
State Bank, B2
State Capitol, A3
State Legislative Building, B3
Willard Drive, A1&2

Using this map key can you find these different places?

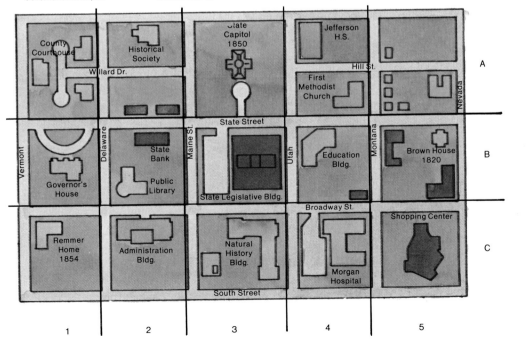

A key number system is helpful to find cities on a big map.

Different cities can be found with such a key.

The cities may be listed on a separate table. Beside each city are the numbers or letters needed to find it on the map.

PHYSICAL MAPS

Some maps show natural land and water forms. Such maps are called physical, or topographic, maps. One kind of physical map is the relief map. A relief map looks something like

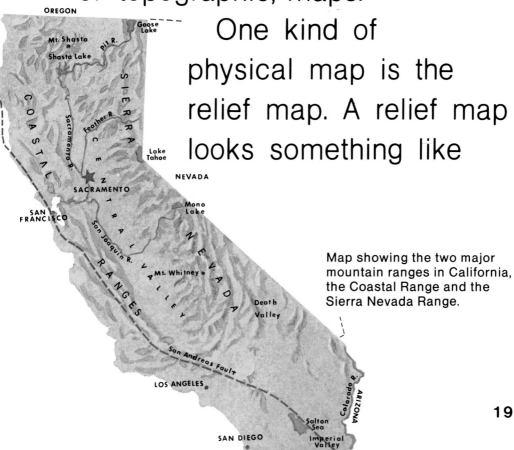

Map showing the two major mountain ranges in California, the Coastal Range and the Sierra Nevada Range.

a picture taken from above. It shows forms such as mountains and rivers.

Another kind of physical map is the contour map. Contours are lines drawn on maps along equal lines

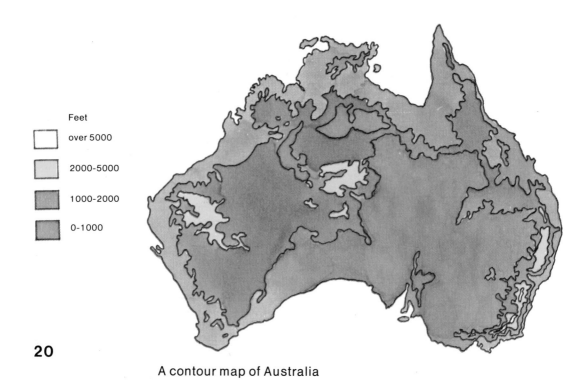

Feet

over 5000

2000-5000

1000-2000

0-1000

A contour map of Australia

of height. The lines show how high the land or mountains are.

Contour lines are a good way of showing height.

A color key can also be used on a contour map.

Colors are used to show how high the land or mountains are.

A color key is used to show the difference in heights.

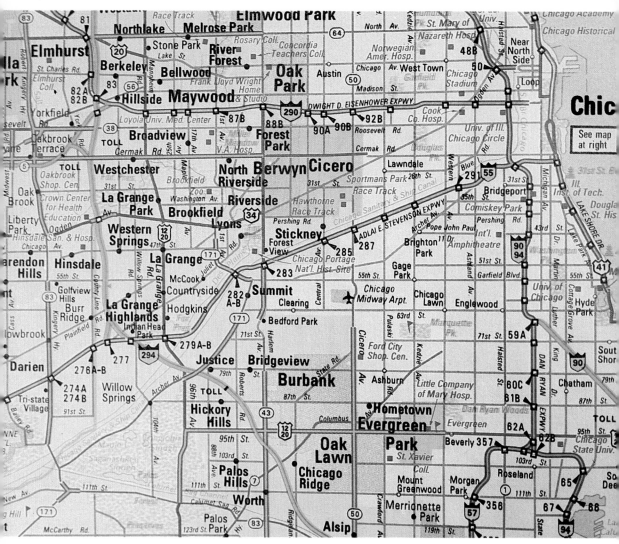

City map showing a section of Chicago

SPECIAL KINDS OF MAPS

Maps can be made to show special kinds of things.

One kind of special map is a road map.

A road map of the United States shows the main roads in the country.

A state road map shows the roads in that state.

A city road map shows streets in a city.

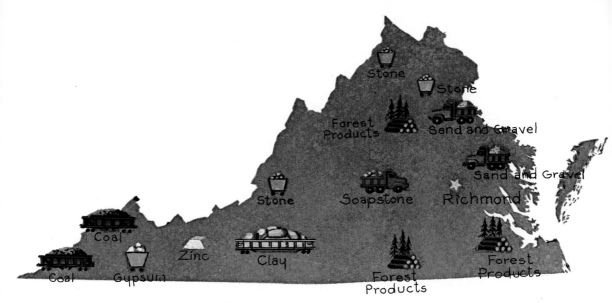

Natural resource map of Virginia

Forests and minerals are found in nature. They are called natural resources.

Natural resources can be shown on a map. A natural resources map has a key or shows symbols on the map.

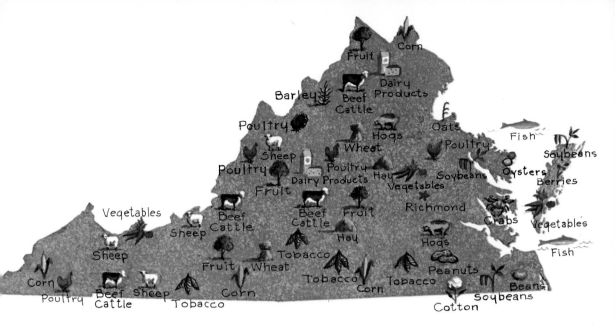

Products map of Virginia

A products map shows such things as vegetables, fruits, and animals raised or used for food.

A products map has a key or shows symbols right on the map. Sometimes it will also show natural resources.

25

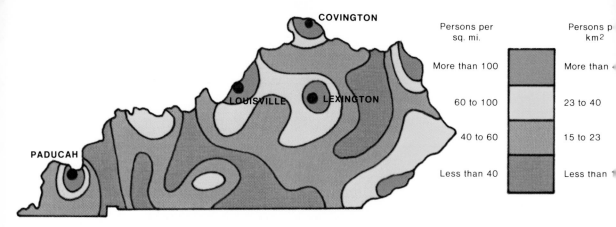

Population map of Kentucky

The total number of people who live in an area is called a population.

In certain parts of an area there will be more people than in others. A population density map shows how many people live in an area.

A population density map uses a color key.

26

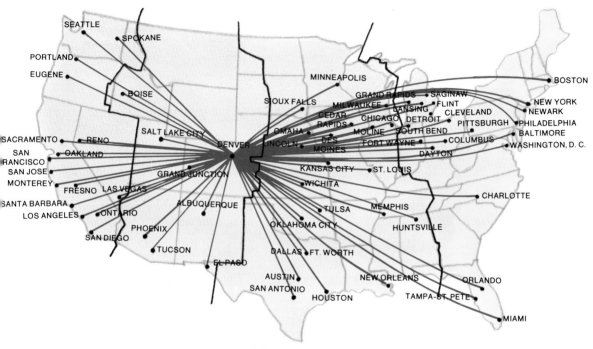

Map showing cities serviced by an airline

Many people travel in airplanes run by airlines.

Airline maps show what cities an airline flies to.

Not all airlines fly to the same cities, so each airline has its own map.

Pilots who fly planes use maps also. When flying low, a pilot uses a ground map. On it the pilot finds things that can be seen easily from the air.

Lines that separate one state or country from another are called boundaries. Boundaries are shown on political maps.

Many political maps show states or countries in different colors. Political maps change when boundaries change.

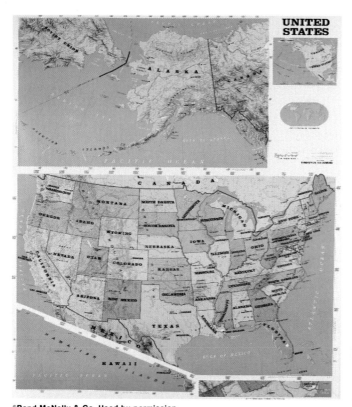

UNITED STATES

©Rand McNally & Co. Used by permission.

Left: Map of the 50 states in the United States.

Below: Map of the countries in the world

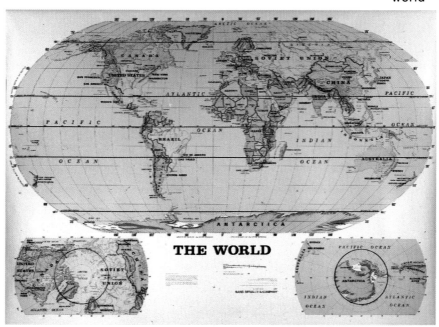

THE WORLD

©Rand McNally & Co. Used by permission.

29

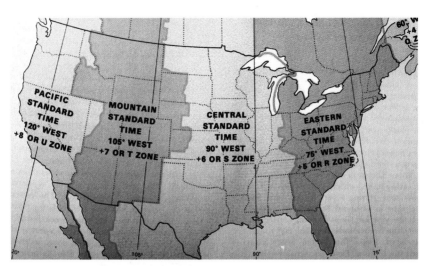

Time zone map of the United States

There are different time zones around the world. They are shown on a time zone map.

There is one hour's difference between zones that are side by side.

You can find out about the ocean floor from an ocean floor map.

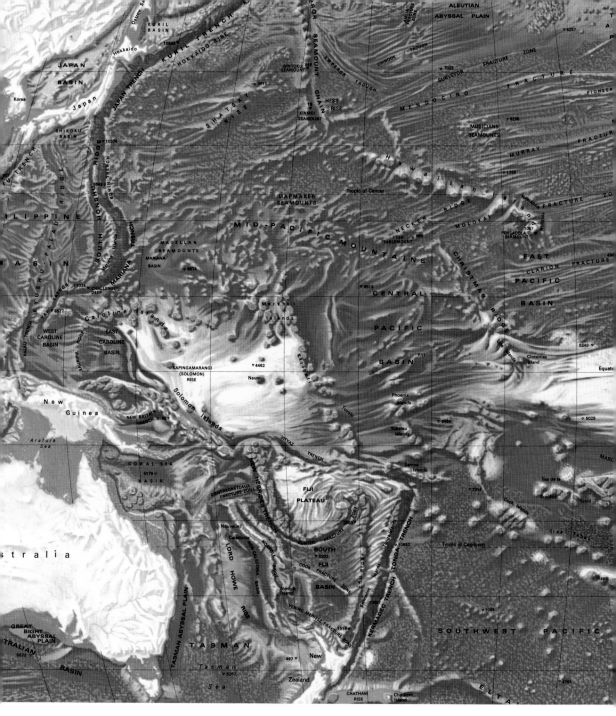

This is a map of a section of the Pacific Ocean floor.
You can see there are valleys and mountains. Some
islands are the tips of mountains that rise above the water.

©Rand McNally & Co., R.L. 83-S-109

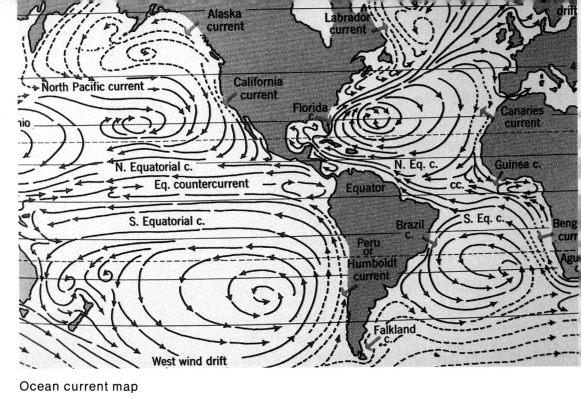

Ocean current map

The water in oceans is always moving. Some of the water always moves in a certain direction.

Such moving water is called a current. A current is something like a river in an ocean.

There are different currents in the oceans of the world. They can be shown on an ocean current map.

A nautical chart is used by people traveling by boat or ship.

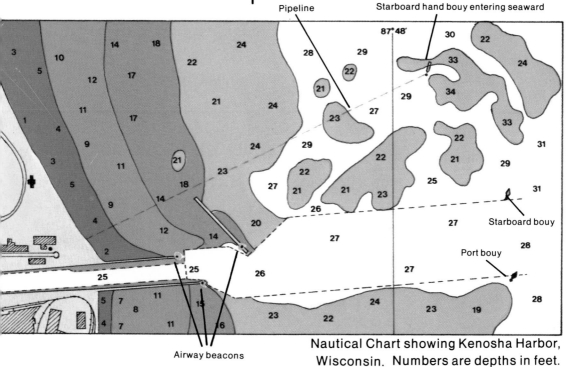

Nautical Chart showing Kenosha Harbor, Wisconsin. Numbers are depths in feet.

Water depths are shown at different places along the shoreline.

Some other things shown on a nautical chart are buoys and underwater rocks.

Weather maps are used by people both on land and at sea.

A weather map shows such things as temperature, wind speed, rain, and snow.

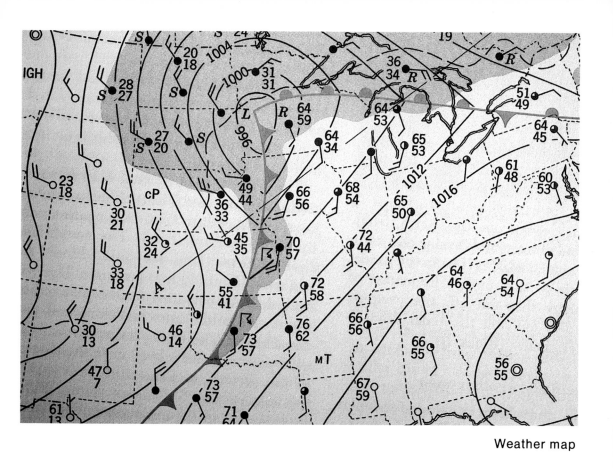

Weather map

The weather in different parts of a country can be shown.

It is important to use the map key to read a weather map correctly.

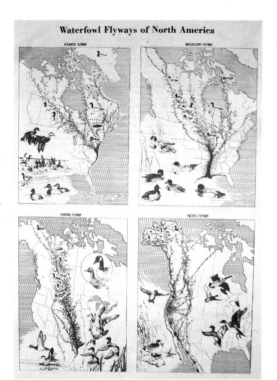

Birds and many other animals move when the weather changes. Their movements or migration patterns can be shown on a map.

Some kinds of birds migrate in spring and fall. They travel along paths called flyways. Flyways can be shown on a map.

An isometric map is fun to look at.

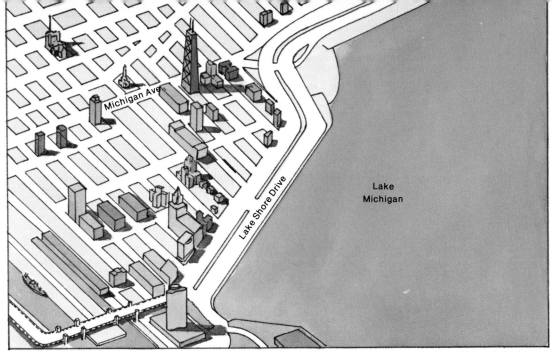

Michigan Ave

Lake Shore Drive

Lake
Michigan

An isometric map of a section of Chicago

Figures on it are drawn so that three dimensions are shown: length, width, and height.

On an isometric map of a city you can compare the heights of the different buildings.

The planet Earth is shown on many kinds of maps. Other planets and moons can be shown on maps also.

Our moon has mountains and craters. Many of them have been named. These landforms and others are shown on a moon map.

To find your way around the night sky you need a map called a star chart.

Some of the stars seem to belong together in

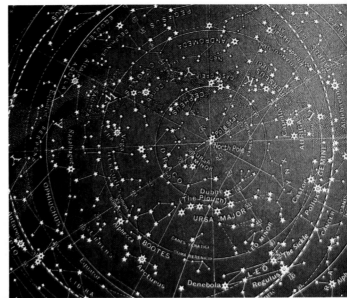

Left: Map of the moon showing the five
possible landing sites selected
for the first manned landing
on the moon by the Apollo 11.
Above: Star chart. The Big Dipper
is in Ursa Major. The Little
Dipper is in Ursa Minor.

groups. Such star groups
are called constellations.

The Big Dipper and the
Little Dipper are two well-
known constellations.

AN ATLAS

An old Greek legend
tells about some giants
called Titans.

The Titans were defeated
in battle by the Greek
gods. All the Titans were
then punished.

One of them was named
Atlas. His punishment was
to hold the world on his
shoulders.

Old maps made
hundreds of years ago
showed a drawing of Atlas

Statue of Atlas carrying the world on his shoulders

holding the world on his shoulders.

That is why a book of maps is called an atlas. An atlas is a collection of different kinds of maps.

A GLOBE

A globe is a model of Earth. It is shaped like the Earth. All the land and water on Earth are shown on a globe. Everything is drawn to scale.

A globe shows the world as a whole. It does not show small areas in detail.

Details can be shown on flat maps. There are many kinds of flat maps.

Shapes and distances on

Globe

flat maps aren't as exact
as those on a globe.

That is because a globe
is shaped like Earth. Flat
maps aren't.

Celestial globe

Terrestrial globe

A globe showing the Earth is called a terrestrial globe. It shows land and water.

A globe showing the heavens is called a celestial globe. It shows stars, moons, and planets.

CARTOGRAPHY

The science of making maps is called cartography.

A person who makes maps is a cartographer.

A cartographer sometimes uses photos to help make a map. Such photos can be taken from airplanes or satellites.

A map must be drawn carefully. So a cartographer works carefully.

Cartography is a science.

WORDS YOU SHOULD KNOW

airline map(AIR • lyne MAP)—a map that shows plane flights

atlas(AT • lis)—a collection of different kinds of maps

boundary(BOUND • ree)—a line that separates one state or country from another

cardinal directions(KAR • din • el dih • REK • shunz)—North, South, East, West

cartographer(kar • TOG • rah • fer)—a person who makes maps

cartography(kar • TOG • rah • fee)—the science of map-making

celestial globe(seh • LES • shil)—a model of the heavens

contour map(KAHN • toor • MAP)—a map that shows height

current(KER • ent)—part of a body of water that moves faster than the water around it

globe(GLOAB)—a sphere that is a model of something like Earth

ground map(GROUND MAP)—a map pilots use when flying low to identify things on the ground

intermediate directions(in • ter • MEE • dee • yet dih • REK • shunz)—Northeast, Northwest, Southeast, Southwest

isometric map(eye • soh • MET • rik MAP)—a map that shows dimensions of length, width, height

key(KEE)—the part of a map that contains such things as symbols and scale to read the map

legend(leh • jend)—see key

map(MAP)—a drawing, usually on a flat surface, of a place

map key number system—a way of finding places on a map

migration map(my • GRAY • shun MAP)—a map that shows paths animals take when seasons change

moon map—a map that shows the natural features of the moon

natural resources map(NAT • cher • el REE • sor • ses MAP)—a map that shows such things as minerals and forests with symbols

nautical chart(NAW • tick • el CHART)—a map that is used by a person traveling on water

ocean current map(oh • shen KER • rent) — a map that shows the paths currents follow

ocean floor map — a map that shows such things as valleys and mountains at the bottom of an ocean

outline — a line showing the boundary of something on a map

political map(poh • LIT • ih • kel) — a map that shows boundaries of states and countries

population density map (pop • yoo • lay • shun DEN • sih • tee) — a map that shows where people live

products map(PRAH • duckts) — a map that shows by symbols what people raise in an area

physical map(FIH • zi • kel) — a map that shows natural land and water forms

relief map(re • LEEF) — a map that looks something like a picture taken from above

road map(RODE) — a map that shows different kinds of roads in a country, state, or city

scale(SKAIL) — a system by which real distances can be shown by much smaller distances

star chart — a map on which constellations are shown

symbol(SIM • bel) — a figure that stands for something else

terrestrial globe(ter • REST • chel) — a model of Earth

time zone map — a map that shows boundaries between areas having a time difference

weather map — a map that shows weather conditions

INDEX

About the Author

Ray Broekel is a full-time freelance writer who lives with his wife Peg and a dog, Fergus, in Ipswich, Massachusetts. He has had twenty years of experience as a children's book editor and newspaper supervisor, and has taught many subjects in kindergarten through college levels. Dr. Broekel has had over 1,000 stories and articles published, and over 100 books. His first book was published in 1956 by Childrens Press.